PUFFINS

Printed in Hong Kong

99 00 01 02 03 5 4 3 2 1

Library of Congress Cataloging-in-Publication Data
Taylor, K. (Kenneth), 1954–
    Puffins / Kenny Taylor.
        p. cm. — (World life library)
        ISBN 0-89658-419-4
        1. Puffins. I. Title. II. Series.
QL696.C42T29 1999   98-51771
598.3'3–dc21   CIP

Distributed in Canada by Raincoast Books, 8680 Cambie Street, Vancouver, B.C. V6P 6M9

Published by Voyageur Press, Inc.
123 North Second Street, P. O. Box 338, Stillwater, MN 55082, U.S.A.
651-430-2210, fax 651-430-2211

Educators, fundraisers, premium and gift buyers, publicists and marketing managers: Looking for creative products and new sales ideas? Voyageur Press books are available at special discounts when purchased in quantities, and special editions can be created to your specifications. For details contact the marketing department at 800-888-9653.

Photographs copyright © 1999 by

Front cover © Colin Baxter
Back cover © Tom & Pat Leeson
Page 1 © Harry M Walker
Page 4 © Alissa Crandall
Page 6 © Kenneth Day
Page 9 © Kenny Taylor
Page 11 © Stephen Krasemann (NHPA)
Page 12 © Alissa Crandall
Page 15 © Jeff Foott
Page 16 © Tom & Pat Leeson
Page 19 © Tom Vezo (BBC Natural History Unit)
Page 20 © Colin Baxter
Page 22 © Tom & Pat Leeson
Page 23 © Harry M Walker
Page 24 © Andy Rouse (NHPA)
Page 27 © Colin Baxter

Page 28 © Kenny Taylor
Page 32 © Kenny Taylor
Page 35 © Jean-Louis Le Moigne (NHPA)
Page 36 © Kenny Taylor
Page 38 © Kenny Taylor
Page 39 Top Left © Bill Coster (NHPA)
Page 39 Top Right © Kenneth Day
Page 39 Bottom Left © Laurie Campbell
Page 39 Bottom Right © Laurie Campbell
Page 40 © Kenny Taylor
Page 41 © John Shaw (NHPA)
Page 42 © Martyn Colbeck (Oxford Scientific Films)
Page 45 © Kevin Schafer (NHPA)
Page 46 © Laurie Campbell
Page 49 © Kenny Taylor
Page 50 © Kenny Taylor

Page 52 © Frans Lanting (Minden Pictures)
Page 53 © Pete Oxford (BBC Natural History Unit)
Page 54 © Rob Jordan (Bruce Coleman)
Page 56 © Kenny Taylor
Page 57 © Laurie Campbell
Page 58 © Colin Baxter
Page 61 © Colin Baxter
Page 62 © Kevin Schafer (NHPA)
Page 65 © Kenny Taylor
Page 66 © Colin Baxter
Page 67 © Laurie Campbell
Page 68 © Colin Baxter
Page 69 © Hans Reinhard (Bruce Coleman)
Page 70 © Harry M Walker
Page 72 © Colin Baxter

PUFFINS

Kenny Taylor

WORLDLIFE
LIBRARY

Voyageur Press

Contents

Introduction

Even if you've never seen a puffin in the wild, it's a fair bet that you'll know what one looks like. The general puffin body-plan and summer livery – chunky chest, big and colorful bill, bright feet and dapper plumage – is as familiar to many people as the shape and patterning of pandas and owls.

Product labels, tourist goods, cuddly toys and T-shirts around both Pacific and Atlantic coasts ensure that puffin imagery gets plenty of northern exposure. But all this 'puffinabilia' suggests more than good marketing, for it reflects something deeper.

Puffin appeal may stem, in part, from a subconscious human tendency to react positively to creatures which have babyish proportions and roundedness. Mix in bold colors, from hot oranges to jet black, and the visual attraction builds. Add motion, from rolling, Chaplinesque walks to the subtlest eye movements, and the allure is heightened even more. But there's the puzzle, for most people have never been within scent or sound of a puffin colony, let alone got close enough to marvel at the complexities of close-range puffin communication. Yet the image is powerful, the birds important to millions. They have become an icon of something more than just the sum of features, colors and movements. Perhaps even their very inaccessibility has given them an extra cachet.

Like rainforests, tigers or great whales, it's good to know, quite simply, that puffins exist and that through their existence, they reveal something of the health of the oceans. Remove puffins from the sum of life, and a major alarm would sound about the health of the planet. Some dazzling sparks of northern hemisphere vibrancy would be extinguished.

The purpose of this book is to reveal some facets of the current, healthy

Dapper fishing ace – the classic puffin look.

brightness of world puffindom. This information stems from studies carried out over several decades by myself and a fairly small band of other people who have been lucky enough to live beside puffins and explore some aspects of their feeding, breeding and behavior for long periods of time. Almost all of this research work has been done on land during spring and summer months, with virtually none during other seasons. This is not because puffinologists are a particular class of fair-weather ornithologist; rather, it reflects the sheer physical challenge of studying puffins. This includes the near impossibility of seeing much of them at all outside their breeding season, when they disperse widely at sea, and can be extremely tricky to locate on winter boat trips.

Most of the world's major puffinries are hard places to reach, even in calm weather. Think of a place like the islands of St Kilda, the ultimate puffin super-colony in Britain and Ireland. Almost 100 miles (160 km) out west from the Scottish mainland, and a good 37 miles (60 km) clear of its main Outer Hebridean neighbors to the east, St Kilda sits in rugged ocean isolation.

Close to the main track of storms in this part of the North Atlantic, the four principal islands and craggy outcrops which make up the St Kilda archipelago are battered by seas which can pile waves as high as tall buildings, and pummelled by gales which can rip heavy radar equipment from its mountings. That's in summer. In winter, the noise of boulders being hurled against each other by raging water could deafen those who once inhabited St Kilda's deserted village.

But the continental shelf sits not far from here, as the seabird flies, so there is tremendous mixing of food-rich water to fuel the productivity of marine life. The islands themselves help to stir the mix, as currents divide and stream past them, swirl back together and keep the oceanic broth on the cool bubble in spring and summer.

These are some of the things which make such a place so good for seabirds, Atlantic puffins included. But they are also features which make

*Most puffins live in huge
colonies, tens of thousands strong.*

St Kilda a place on the outer limits for most people. Once there, you savor the experience all the more for it being precarious: a privilege granted in part through temporary blessings of favorable weather.

What applies to St Kilda holds true for the majority of the world's really large puffinries, be they in Atlantic or Pacific. Think of Buldir Island, most isolated of the Aleutian chain which stretches between Alaska and Siberia. A mere speck of land, more than 60 miles (100 km) clear of Kiska to the east, it holds three volcanic peaks, rising above hills which roll down to beaches of boulders and gravel beneath high slopes and above vertical cliffs. Out from the island, thick beds of brown kelp stretch for half a mile (0.5 km). To either side, fantastically strong flows of water in major 'passes' which link the Bering Sea to the Pacific swirl the marine mix. It rains a lot here, and then some. But auks love it. Twelve different kinds breed here, including tufted and horned puffins, making it the world's most diverse breeding place for this characterful family.

Think further about the islands at the tip of the Lofoten chain in Norway; the Westmanns in Iceland; Talan Island in the Sea of Okhotsk; these and many other major colonies take time, perseverance and good luck for a would-be puffin-watcher to visit. So even the details now recorded about puffin life, in the few months when they spend part of the day ashore at colonies, have taken a huge amount of effort to obtain.

For the wider picture of what puffins do at sea, both within and beyond the breeding season, the information for all species is scanty. There is precious little known about what puffins do in the watery element which supports them for much of their lives, and about how they spend the majority of the year when they are away from their colonies. So there is still much to learn and much, perhaps, that we'll never know. And that sense of continuing mystery, linked to some of the world's most familiar-seeming seabirds, is another powerful part of that old puffin magic.

Meet the Trio

Puffins are members of the auk family. This 24-species-strong group includes an impressive array of birds. These range from the diminutive 3 oz (85 g) least auklet (the males of which, amazingly, have testes bigger than their brains) to the chunky Brunnich's guillemot, or thick-billed murre as it is known in North America, which weighs-in at around 2 lb (0.9 kg). The largest member of the family in recent history – the great auk – would have been four or five times heavier. But mass slaughter for meat and feathers floored that heavyweight. The final push to extinction for the great auk came, ironically, from museums greedy to grab a good specimen for their collections before it was too late, thereby inflating prices and encouraging the slaughter of the last survivors in 1844.

Auks are typical seabirds, which in turn are an élite band of little more than 300 species out of the world's grand bird tally of more than 8000 species. As is usual for seabirds, auks take several years to reach maturity. Most auks, including all puffins, lay just one egg a year, but usually enjoy quite high breeding success. Adult survival from year to year can also be high, so that they have fairly long lives relative to most birds (25 years or more in the case of the Atlantic puffin).

Such life history details have been shaped by the rigors of survival in and around a tricky environment – the ocean – where food may be plentiful in places, but hard to pinpoint, and the forces of weather on the surface and the pressures and difficulties of foraging in poorly lit water below are too demanding for all but the few hundred specialist seabirds to cope.

All puffins look striking in their summer breeding finery. But perhaps the most amazing of all is the tufted puffin (*Fratercula cirrhata*). Largest of the world puffin trio, it also has the broadest geographical spread, north to south, of any member of the auk family. Weighing in at more than 1 lb 12 oz (0.8 kg),

Here's looking at you: a pair of tufted puffins.

males are slightly larger than females, a principle which holds good for all puffins. There's just no mistaking the tufted puffin when it's ready for big-time colony socializing. Its plumage is almost entirely black, with a sheen when the feathering is fresh which gives real gloss. The black extends high up the side of the tufted puffin's head. And it is there that grand evolutionary design master-strokes come in. A curving, clean-drawn line separates the dark plumage from the chalk-white of the face, the white becoming the dominant feature of the bird's plumage, save for a black cap, over the front half of the head.

At the back of the head, two ivory-colored plumes of feathers arc up and trail down to the base of the neck. By turns, these can appear regal, in a lion-ish way; ethereal, when the near-constant breeze (or gale) at a puffinry blows them this way and that; or punk, when seawater clings and they stand out in stiff spikes to the side.

After this visual plumage feast, the rest is a bonus. The beak is massive, red-dish-orange for the most part, but with olive-yellow on the third of the upper mandible nearest the head. A yellow iris (unlike the dark eyes of horned and Atlantic puffins) is a neat touch, drawing the eye of the beholder in to a pin-point focus on that remarkable head. A pale 'rosette' of soft flesh at the bill's base, orange eye-ring and puffin trademark orange-red feet are the finishing touches to this arresting blend of color, line and form.

Tufted puffins live throughout the so-called 'boreal' and 'low Arctic' areas of the North Pacific. You can find them from Big Sur in California, around and over the Pacific top in the Aleutian Islands and down to Hokkaido in Japan. But they are most abundant in the central part of this ocean-rim domain, from British Columbia through Alaska and south to the Sea of Okhotsk. In Alaska, tufted puffins are believed to be one of the state's most numerous seabirds, with a population estimated in millions.

A tufted puffin brings in the catch.

Horned and Atlantic puffins can move stiff ornaments above
their eyes for subtle, close-range signalling. Yellow rosettes of skin at the
base of the bill are sometimes nibbled in courtship, perhaps to stimulate a partner.

Epicenter of tufted puffindom is the eastern end of the Aleutian chain, not far from the Alaska Peninsula, especially on islands which lie beside the major marine passes linking the Bering Sea and the Pacific. Here, the area around the Akutan and Unimak Passes may hold as many as one million breeding tufteds, with some 163,000 at Egg Island – the largest known colony. The meeting of oceans at these passes brings food particles, which might otherwise drop to the seabed, close to the surface. These, in turn, feed small fish, which feed bigger fish, seabirds, seals, sea lions and whales.

If a mix of crazy flamboyance and cool lines is part of what gives tufted puffins their allure, a different kind of overstatement and restraint distinguishes the horned puffin (*Fratercula corniculata*). The bird takes its name from a dark fleshy 'horn' which sits above each eye.

Rising just clear of the top of its head, the horned puffin's high-rise lashes can move as its eye rings raise or lower, adding emphasis to the bird's expression. Couple this with a mascara-like line trailing back from behind the eye to the rear of the head, set against a ground of china-white head feathers, and the effect is astonishing.

There's no escaping the correspondence, to a human observer, between the look of these birds and facial make-up of classical Japanese 'Noh' play performers. This comparison is not gratuitous – a case of squeezing another species into human garb just for our amusement – but hints at the real power of the horned puffin's ornaments as signalling devices.

For all puffins, close-range signalling which emphasizes certain colors and body structures is an important part of social communication. So the correspondence with some human display devices, rather than being trivial, suggests instead a parallel evolution of patterns, with the seabird player in the display game hitting on the design a few million years before the human performers.

The sheer size of the horned puffin's bill in relation to its head is remarkable. This makes it seem an even more striking appendage than the bills sported by tufted and Atlantic puffins, spectacular though these are, and means that the horned is the ultimate 'sea parrot' of world puffindom.

The main part of a horned puffin's bill is buttery yellow, with a clear divide between this and an outer, brick-orange section. Seen against the sun, the paler part of the bill lets some light shine through, giving a clue to its impermanence in the annual puffin scheme of things. Puffin bills are made of keratin, the same substance that forms human fingernails and toenails. The Cyrano-de-Bergerac-rivalling beakware is a concoction for spring and summer colony life, formed from sheaths of keratin flushed with pigment, which grow over a smaller, duller beak structure which the puffin keeps year-round.

The Atlantic puffin (*Fratercula arctica*) is the smallest of the world bunch. At almost 14 in (35 cm) in body length, it is a full 2 in (5 cm) shorter and a good 6 oz (200 g) lighter than the tufted puffin. But size isn't everything, as the Atlantic puffin's summer appearance demonstrates.

Compared with its Pacific-dwelling relatives, the Atlantic puffin's features are modest. The bill, though colorful, seems in neat proportion to the head size, and the whole impression is of a compact design and dapper appearance.

It's the addition of a smoky-blue panel, outlined in pale, creamy-yellow, which gives the Atlantic puffin's bill a subtle beauty, as opposed to the strong, bold coloring of its cousins. This color scheme emphasizes the buttercup tones of the fleshy rosette all the more, with a subtle contrast of charcoal feathering on the lower cheeks as further fine detail.

The Atlantic puffin's eye ornaments are no match for the horned's in size, but the bird can use them to great expressive effect when seen at close range. The vibrantly orange, webbed feet set the whole breeding 'kit' off to advantage.

This can lead to some intriguing questions, relevant to all three puffin species: why do male and female puffins look virtually identical (although females are a little bit smaller than males, on average) and why do both sexes have such flamboyant breeding season finery? What could be the forces which

have acted, over tens of thousands of puffin lifespans, to shape and tint the structures and colors which define the modern puffin – be it horned, tufted or Atlantic – and which make each species so attractive to the human eye?

A further puzzle is why, within the auk family, there should be a pronounced difference in the degree of breeding season flamboyance adopted by different species. As a family, the auks have a surprising number of species which grow dramatic beak- and head-feather structures in the breeding season.

Recent studies of the genetic make-up of the family split it into two major groups. One of these includes the murres, black guillemots and all murrelets. The other includes the auklets and puffins. Not one of the 15 species in the first group has a brightly colored outer covering to its bill (although many do have very colorful bill linings) and only two murrelets sport ornamental head plumes. However, nearly all the members of the puffin-auklet bunch have a brightly colored bill which gains extra plates during the breeding season, and all except Cassin's auklet have dramatic facial ornaments such as plumes.

For puffins, the strongest potential explanation for the equal finery of males and females stems from Charles Darwin's theory of evolution. Keystone of this is 'natural selection', the gradual shifting and shaping of species through the survival advantages given to offspring by particular body structures and behavior.

One aspect of Darwin's ideas which is very relevant to the look of puffins and other ornamented auks is known as 'sexual selection'. This works through mating success. The idea is that if one sex prefers certain features in a mate, and if mates chosen for such qualities enjoy better breeding performance than others, then such features (although still varying from individual to individual) will become normal for the chosen sex. A striking and extreme case of this is the peacock, where female choice of males with big, colorful tails is likely to have been the driving force behind the gradual development of the biggest,

An Atlantic puffin in grass well fertilized by puffin guano.

brightest male tails of any bird. But what about puffins?

Since both puffin sexes probably work just as hard and in broadly, though not exactly, similar ways to rear their young in a tough environment, the qualities a female puffin seeks in a mate may be similar to those a male puffin desires in a female. Structures which evolve though sexual selection do not need to have an everyday function. Indeed, something as bulky and flamboyant as a peacock tail probably handicaps a male. But it demonstrates quality, nevertheless. If you're a hale and hearty male peacock with a great-looking tail, you're probably in good shape and pretty smart at avoiding enemies.

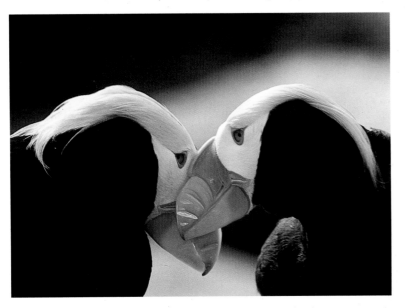

Billing is a noisy greeting and pairing display.

For puffins, it is interesting that part of their breeding ornamentation – the beak – does have a direct use in digging, fighting and food gathering. But the sheer size of beak is greater than necessary for any of these activities (puffins get enough food in winter with much narrower beaks, for example). Other head ornaments – whether plumes, horns or eye-rings – seem to function only in display. They could be the peacock-tail equivalents of the puffin world.

Evidence that both males and females of one species of auk like the look of the same adornments has been found by behavior researchers Ian Jones and Fiona Hunter. Working on remote, auk-packed Buldir Island in the Aleutians, they discovered that both male and female crested auklets prefer relatively long head-crests when choosing a potential mate. No one yet knows

such fine details of what puffins find appealing, but future studies of such matters could reap interesting scientific rewards.

By the end of a hard season's fishing, fighting and hob-nobbing with mate and neighbors, puffin beak sheaths show signs of wear, and may even slough off while the birds are still visiting the land. Native peoples in the Pacific north-west and Aleutians knew this, and collected beaks for use in their own rituals. They could also get fresher beaks from harvesting large numbers of puffins for food, at which time tufted puffin plumes could also be removed for later use as ornaments on tribal clothing: Inuit people used to make cosy, feather-lined parkas using tufted-puffin skins. Strung together, puffin beaks would rattle – a big audio boon for shamans in ceremonies where seabirds might figure as spirit helpers. Hundreds of beaks were used on the outside of garments worn by some Inuit or Aleuts in the Bering Sea area, or set to great ornamental effect against bold woven designs in costumes such as blankets worn by Chilkat dancers. But it was the chest coloring, rather than the body ornaments, which led one group of Inuit to call this bird 'katukh-puk', meaning 'big white breast', as this is a good way of distinguishing horned and tufted puffins from a distance.

The orange-red part of a puffin's bill gives a rough clue to its age. All three species develop prominent grooves in these zones as they grow. Grooves can be quite easy to see through binoculars or telescope, since they often look whiter than the rest of the bill. For the Atlantic puffin, studies of individually rec-ognizable birds, banded with metal and plastic leg-rings for the purpose of pop-ulation research, have shown that almost all puffins of breeding age have two or more bill grooves. Immature birds generally have less than two. So if you see a bird with several bill grooves, it is almost certain that it is five years old or more. Trouble is, puffin grooves don't keep accumulating like growth rings on a tree, and tend only to go to a maximum of three-and-a-bit. So that three-groover

Several grooves along the upper bill show that this bird is a full adult.

seen through a telescope could be five, 20, or perhaps even 30 years old.

Horned and tufted puffins overlap in about half of their breeding range, but horned puffins also breed farther north than tufted, and tufted breed farther south. The southern limit of horned-puffin breeding on the North American shores of the Pacific is British Columbia. From there, it gradually comes more into its own, working north and west along the Alaska Peninsula and the Aleutians, although it is much less numerous than the tufted puffin in the eastern Aleutians. Coasts and islands in the Bering and Chuckchi Seas and down eastern Siberia to the Sea of Okhotsk are within its breeding domain.

The largest colony in Asia is on Talan Island. More than 100,000 horned puffins share this small, treeless island off the Siberian coast with a variety of other auks. The world stronghold of the horned puffin is the Semidi Islands in the Gulf of Alaska. Together, these rugged, tussock-grass-covered islands may hold some 350,000 breeders, with Suklik Island alone giving breeding space to a quarter of a million.

The breeding range of Atlantic puffins encompasses a huge slice of their namesake ocean and beyond, from the high Arctic in Svalbard in the north, to the relatively mild and humid islands in the Gulf of Maine far to the south. On the basis of body measurements, zoologists recognize three different types or 'sub-species' within the Atlantic puffin's realm.

The commonest and most widespread type is *Fratercula arctica arctica*, which breeds from Maine to north-east Canada, and in eastern Greenland, Iceland and Norway. Its total population could be more than 10 million birds, making it the most abundant kind of puffin on the planet.

Smaller, and with a more angular bill, is *Fratercula arctica grabae*, the kind of puffin found from the Faroe Islands to France, including Britain and Ireland. Latest estimates show that some 1.5 million birds belong to this subspecies.

Rarest and least known of all the world's puffin types is *Fratercula arctica naumannii*, largest of the Atlantic puffins, which is scattered in small numbers

Like most seabirds, puffins may take several years
before they begin to breed. Staking a claim to a nesting place and
finding food for a fast-growing chick can be tough, so time off to rest is a bonus.

in Svalbard and north-east Greenland. There may only be a few thousand of these high Arctic, cliff-crevice dwellers, and no ornithologist has so far been able to make a study of them.

Within the broad sweep of Atlantic puffindom, certain breeding areas stand out. At the extremity is Iceland, easily the world puffin center in numerical terms, with a multi-million-strong breeding population. So huge are some of the colonies, in places like the Westmann Islands and north-east Iceland, that numbers can only be broad approximations for the foreseeable future.

Other places are prominent elsewhere: the islands of the St Kilda group, as already discussed, are home to the bulk of British and Irish puffins; colonies in Arctic Norway provide summer dwelling for hundreds of thousands of birds; the islands in Newfoundland's Witless Bay are main breeding grounds for the majority of Atlantic puffins in North America. Those at the other end of the scale – the tiny colonies of only a handful of pairs – seem to thrive despite the lack of social hurly-burly which is the norm for the average puffin, Atlantic, tufted or horned. Coming upon such a place, where the colony life is relaxed and the puffins noticeable for their scarcity rather than force of numbers, can be a bonus on boat trips around the northern fringes of the Atlantic or Pacific. It adds yet another facet to the puffin attraction you may have thought you knew well, but which can still pull some wonderful surprises.

An overview of the familiar look and broad geographical sweep of world puffins would not be complete without a passing nod at a fourth species. The rhinoceros auklet, *Cerorhinca monocerata*, or 'rhino' as some Pacific birders affectionately know it, is so close in body structure to the 'true' puffins of the *Fratercula* group that some taxonomists do class it as a puffin. Indeed, recent analysis of its DNA and proteins adds weight to the body-structure evidence that the rhino is a very close relative of the true puffins. But there are also enough differences in

Newfoundland is one of the few places where Atlantic puffins burrow among trees.

both appearance and behavior to set the rhino a little bit apart, suggesting that it is a kind of bridging species, which links the auklets and the true puffins.

The rhino doesn't have a rounded head or massive bill, and tends to squat down on land much more than true puffins, resting horizontally on the top of its legs. Rhinos are clumsy walkers, often running to maintain momentum. And they usually visit their colonies under cover of darkness.

Named for the upright 'horn' at the base of its upper mandible, the rhino is an intriguing-looking bird, with streaks of white plumage above and below its eyes, set against a general dark, brownish-charcoal to add dramatic emphasis to the appearance of its head. Found from California to the north of Japan, it overlaps with tufted and horned puffins over a major part of its range. Indeed, it may have had some of its breeding behavior shaped by competition with the bigger, heavier tufted puffin.

Observers on the Farallone Islands in California believe that tufted puffins go out of their way to respond to any rhinoceros auklet they see on the shore. The puffins, typically, advance on the auklets until the latter leave. This has led Californian researchers to suggest that rhinos might even have become nocturnal to avoid interference from tufted puffins, and that their choice of nests under forest canopies (which are disliked by tufteds) could also result from this competition. This idea could reward further exploration. Very little is known about the postures, movements and the way of using head ornaments in this species (which tends to be much more audibly vocal when ashore than true puffins). Anyone intrigued by rhino-puffin links and some unsolved seabird questions could find fertile ground for study in the colonies of this widespread, but somewhat mysterious, Pacific seabird. But for the purposes of this book, the rhino will now have to bow out after its honorable mention as a close cousin of the true puffin clan.

A bulky body is good for diving but makes for energetic flying.

Putting on the Puffin Style

Each spring, puffins go through a remarkable transformation in appearance and behavior. For seven months, they ride out the storms of autumn and winter, alone or in small groups, far from land.

Their appearance is drab. Black and gray are the dominant feather tones all over their body, save for a pale brown zone on the head for tufted and everywhere except chest, belly and under-tail in horned and Atlantic puffins. Legs are an insipid yellow, beaks amber in tufteds and dull brown and red, or gray-blue and red, in horned and Atlantic. Bill size, though large, is nowhere near as remarkable as in the breeding season. This is how puffins look for a major part of the year. But almost no one sees them then, so it's the colorful highlights which stick in the mind and help to define the image of the three species.

As days lengthen and increasing warmth coaxes the year's first flush of marine food production in northern seas, puffins shed the wintry mono-chromes and hit the Technicolor. Bill plates re-grow, tinted with red, yellow, cream, toffee or blue-gray and fuse to give the familiar, parrot-like profile. Other pigments pump a spring flamboyance from sleek heads to 'pass-the-sunglasses' feet, from bright eye-lines to ink-dipped tail tips.

Freshly feathered and painted, the puffins move inshore, gathering in flocks on the water beside their colonies. Off big puffinries, the birds muster in their tens of thousands. To watch this annual gathering at its peak is to see one of the most astonishing signs of spring in the northern hemisphere. By windswept islands and cold northern shores around the rim of both oceans, the scene is transformed.

Months have gone by when these places may have seemed almost empty of life, blasted by squalls, the sparse vegetation browned by wind-chill, salt

Evening is often the time when puffins can relax beside burrows.

spray or snow. Now, the wanderers have returned and the solitary seafarers are set to become sociable land-goers.

Dressed-up for colony life they may be, but for these new arrivals, fresh-in from the open ocean, the sea is still their element of choice, the land an alien territory. Days can pass during which they gather on the water, then depart again without a single puffin having set foot ashore. But the excitement among the water flocks can still be intense, if tricky to see from a human view-point (perhaps through breeze-bounced binoculars from a nearby headland, eyes streaming from the cold). For this is the time when puffins engage in their most obvious courtship.

No one knows if males and females from established pairs stay together outside the breeding season. But once they return to their puffinries, a good deal of male effort is expended making sure that old bonds are re-cemented or new ones attempted, in some cases briefly with more than one female.

Atlantic puffins sometimes attempt to mate on land, but for almost all of them, and for tufted and horned puffins, mating, for preference, has a watery support. Within flocks gathered off a puffinry (from late March onwards for southern ones, weeks later for northern ones), the males seeking such con-summation on the briny waterbed are obvious from their behavior.

A rapid, backward head-flick, repeated many times in succession, is the male's signal of amorous intent. While head-flicking, he tries to maneuver close to a female. If she doesn't dive or fly off, he may turn up the heat of the display, fluttering his wings as he shimmies alongside. Mounting is the culmina-tion of this process, and may last for 20 seconds or more before the couple separates. For duos, which have apparently established themselves as a pair, the two birds continue to swim close to each other in the flock, whether more mating is figuring in the scheme of things or not.

To make the move from sea to land, a regular routine of water and air activity follows. For Atlantic puffins, this begins with small groups of birds

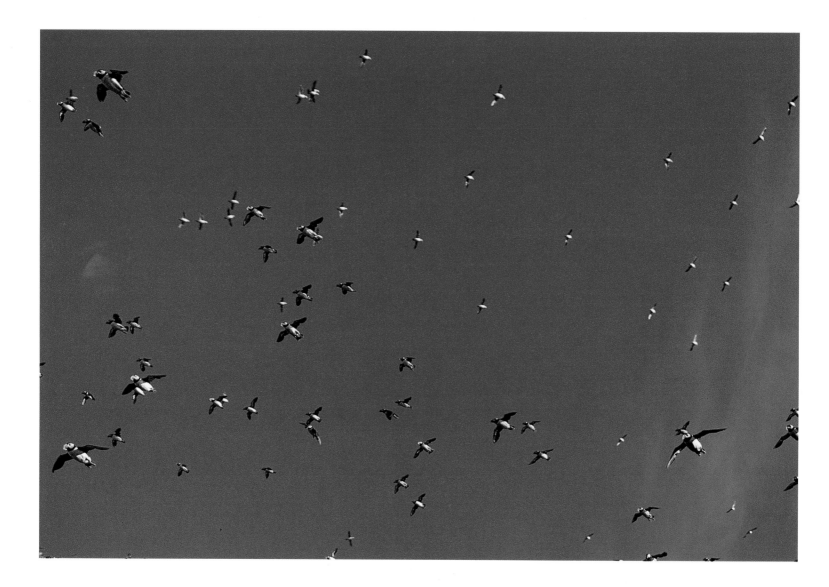

*Flying in a 'wheel' can help an individual puffin to
synchronize its moves to and from a colony with many others. This
cuts the risk of attack by airborne predators and ground-based food pirates.*

merging on the water as numbers swell. The birds' activity changes, with many which were previously snoozing or preening (if they weren't involved in courting) now alert and swimming rapidly. Some puffins take off, flying low passes over the water flocks before splashing down again in flurries of spray.

Gradually, the focus of the flying birds shifts from over the water to over the land. If more join them, the focus locks on the land, with puffins flying in a regular, elliptical track over part of the colony while the birds flocking on the water drift closer and closer to shore. The aerial activity is a 'wheel' – one of the keys to puffin air defences. A puffin can use wheels to move from sea to land and vice versa. It can also join its local wheel to make brief circuits of its home patch, either for casual reconnaissance or when a predator is nearby.

A puffin flying in a wheel follows a set route, which takes it precisely over its own breeding site or favorite grouping place and out over the sea immediately offshore from its part of the colony. At first, the mass of birds on the move in a wheel can make it difficult for the human puffin-watcher to see any method in the mêlée. But careful observation of a single puffin, kept up for a few rounds of a wheel, then repeated with others, can pay dividends by revealing the structure of the whirling roundabout.

The position of a puffin in the air mirrors its desired position on the ground. So by flying a steady course at an appropriate elevation, a wheeling puffin can have repeated chances to choose whether to land, or, if danger threatens, to have another spin. When large numbers of puffins are in a wheel, aerial predators such as great black-backed gulls find it hard to select and home-in on an individual puffin to attack as possible prey.

Finally, a few birds take the plunge. But this time, it's not back into the ocean wave, but for a tentative touchdown on solid ground. The attachment is shaky, and a sudden low sweep from a potential predator can set the whole process back, with evacuation of the slopes and no further landfall attempted that day. Gradually, the need to come ashore for the business of breeding overrides the puffin's urge to stay at sea. For the first time since the previous summer, puffin feet touch the ground, and stay there awhile.

Some birds start by going to their local 'club' – a big rock or tussock where a group of puffins can gather – and meeting some of the neighbors again. Social etiquette has to be observed in joining one of these groups. Landers don't fold their wings immediately on touchdown, but hold them up for a second or two, while leaning forward, bill slightly raised, with one foot placed out in front of the other. This post-landing posture defuses potential aggression from birds already at the club. Immature birds which have not yet learned such club rules tend to find out quickly, through bites from bystanders, that you can't just crash in to such groupings any old how.

Head-jerking is a little-understood display.

At clubs and beside burrows, the most prominent of all puffin behaviors – billing – soon gets into full swing after landfall. At full throttle, billing involves the broadside slapping together of two puffins' bills, producing a noise which can be heard many feet away. Either male or female can invite billing, by making a low approach, head gently swinging from side to side, then touching the lower part of its prospective partner's beak. In Atlantic puffins, a nibble of the partner's fleshy facial rosette can be a further come-on.

Billing, like fighting, is a very popular spectator sport in puffins, and a pair in full bill-banging swing can draw a crowd of onlookers, some of whom may even try to get in on the act. Such intrusion, in turn, may spark a fight, where contestants lock beaks and tussle, each trying to wrong-foot the other.

Carrying a drooping beakload of fish can alert pirates to a good target, so nifty flight moves are vital for puffins to master.

Puffin fights rarely cause obvious
injury. But they look and sound quite
dramatic, as the birds groan and wrench (above).
Small wonder that bill muscles sometimes need exercising (right).

As fairly long-lived birds, which may use the
same burrow or crevice for two decades or more, breeding
puffins get very well acquainted with their near neighbors in a colony.

Burrowing and Fishing

Established pairs in all puffin species have excellent memories of where their burrow or breeding crevice is within a colony. Late snowfalls can mask the entrances to these sites completely, but the puffins still home-in on the spots where they bred in the previous summer. The sight of tufted puffin couples, standing patiently at different parts of a near-featureless snow-covered slope, their dark plumage contrasting with the snowfield as they guard their particular patches of ground and wait for the thaw, is an archetypal serious, yet slightly comic image of puffin life.

Just occasionally, this need to stake fresh claim on old territory can be a puffin's undoing. Following the eruption of a volcano on Heimaey in the Westmann Islands in the early 1970s, some puffins came back in spring, locals told me, landed on hot ash in the places their burrows had been, and perished.

The choice of a breeding site varies a little from species to species. For Atlantic and tufted puffins, family life in a burrow is the norm. But many birds will also use cavities under boulders as nesting shelter, especially in northern colonies, where thin soil cover or late frost could make burrowing difficult.

For horned puffins, crevices on cliffs and chambers under boulders are the normal spring and summer residence. Part of this choice could stem, some believe, from competition for nesting space with the larger tufted puffin. Horned puffins are perfectly able to dig their own burrows, as they do in places such as Kodiak Island. On Puffin Island (one of many so-named in both Pacific and Atlantic) in Kotzebue Sound, Alaska, there are few tufted puffins breeding. Here, most of a large population of horned puffins nest in burrows.

This general separation of nest site, whether forced on horned puffins or not, may be one of the things which allows the two species to coexist over a fair chunk of their ranges. Further ecological space comes between tufted and horned puffins in their choice of both food and feeding area.

It is intriguing, in view of the possible competition and separation between the two Pacific puffins, that tufteds tend to arrive back at their colonies earlier than horned. Perhaps this gives them first crack at the prime puffin sites, although it is also the case that spring cleaning and maintenance of a burrow is a good deal more time- and labor-consuming than re-occupation of a crevice.

In the early part of the nesting season, burrow work is a prominent part of tufted and Atlantic puffins' activities ashore. Both members of a pair share the chores of clearing-out debris, lengthening and modifying tunnels and collecting nest material.

Puffins are expert burrow engineers. They can use their beaks as pick-axes and their sharp-clawed feet as mini-excavators and shovels. A burrow isn't built quickly, and a young pair may have to spend a breeding season or more constructing their breeding place if they have to do it from scratch.

In some places, Atlantic puffins can take over and occupy rabbit burrows. At first sight, this seems surprising, given the puffin's small size in relation to a rabbit. But the rabbit's sensitive nose might be its Achilles heel, so to speak, in underground encounters with a hard-beaked, feisty little opponent, intent on grabbing some subterranean real estate.

Once established, a burrow can be long-lasting, with the option of some early-season improvements if walls have been damaged by winter frosts or spring downpours. Heavy rain on poorly drained sites can be a major problem at some puffinries, flooding burrows and delaying or even preventing egg laying. Squashing of burrows by seals can be another problem, causing collapse of parts of a colony. Some ornithologists believe that seals and sea lions have been a potential major influence shaping where and how a variety of seabirds nest.

Nest lining can keep an egg snug in a damp burrow.

Gathering areas, called 'clubs', are important
in puffin society. Breeders use them to relax off-territory,
and young birds can meet and court possible mates on them.

x

46

In recent decades, pressure from gray seals has reduced puffin breeding areas on the Farne Islands off north-east England. But the Farnes' loss has been the Isle of May's gain. Sitting at the mouth of the Firth of Forth in Scotland, the Isle of May is only part of a day's puffin flight from the Farnes. In the early 1960s, a mere handful of puffin pairs bred here. Then the boom began. Picking up momentum in the 1970s and 1980s and boosted by the rich pickings of herring and sandeels to be caught from nearby waters, the population growth of the Isle of May puffinry became dramatic and rapid. All this has been documented in studies carried out on 'the May' for more than quarter of a century by Professor Mike Harris of the Institute of Terrestrial Ecology at Banchory, Scotland.

I was lucky enough to see some of the stages of this expansion as they happened. From first visits to the May in my early teens, when puffins were confined to slopes and clifftops fringing the island, I saw the birds' fairly speedy spread inland. By the time I was carrying out my own behavioral studies and assisting Mike Harris's monitoring work, puffins from the east and the west sides of the island had worked far enough inland that they faced each other across the island's central track. It looked a bit like a scene where tunnel diggers had made their breakthrough to complete work under the English Channel or Mont Blanc.

Now, more than 20,000 pairs of puffins use the May as their breeding base. Thanks to information provided by ringed birds, we know that at least some of the population growth here has been swelled by immigration from the Farne Islands.

The average tufted or Atlantic puffin's burrow extends more than an adult human's arm-length – perhaps as much as 6½ ft (2 m) – underground. It does not go straight in, mineshaft style, but doglegs so that it often runs only an inch or two below the surface.

Typically, a tunnel is not high enough for a puffin to stand upright, and it is narrow, so that two puffins, making crouched progress in opposite directions, have a bit of a squeeze to get past each other. At the end, a nest chamber opens up, often with enough space for both adults and chick to stand up in, and with a partial lining of grass and feathers. This is the normal bed for the single, off-white egg laid by all puffins. For crevice-nesting horned puffins, and those tufted and Atlantic birds which choose rock-pile residences, soft lining may be shunned altogether, and the egg is simply laid on some loose gravel.

Both male and female puffins share incubation, although there is evidence that female Atlantic puffins put in a longer stint of this than males. The period of egg-warming lasts for six to seven weeks.

As befits their size, incubation is longest in tufted puffins, with an average span of 45 days and an extreme record a fortnight longer. Horned puffins average almost precisely six weeks, Atlantic puffins three days less.

Recently hatched chicks are egg-sized powderpuffs of dark charcoal down. At first, the parents need to brood the chick for it to keep a stable body temperature. But the chick's personal heat control kicks-in after a few days, making prolonged snuggling unnecessary.

For the adults, the chick-rearing period is a time of feverish activity. Both sexes need to make prolonged fishing trips, sometimes many miles out from the colony, to seek and catch beakloads of small fish to satisfy the needs of their growing youngster. Junior, meanwhile, can have a relatively easy time of it, concentrating on digesting the last meal, waiting for the next, and growing.

Chicks in burrows have the added benefit that their own body heat helps to warm the nest chamber. Burrows are energy-efficient dwellings, their insulative cappings of soil and grass reducing heat loss and making the well-drained ones fairly cosy, no matter what the weather may be doing outside. Nor are they totally dark. Chicks can look at their surroundings in dim light that penetrates down the tunnel. One summer, while working with producer Bernard Walton and cameraman Barrie Britton on the BBC TV 'Wildlife on One' film

A powderpuff of downy feathers helps to
keep a puffling warm during the many hours when
it sits alone in a nest chamber, waiting for its next meal.

A chick which has heard a parent's
movements along the burrow tunnel moves to
greet the arrival with lowered head and soft cheeping.

Clowns of the Air, I watched one chick for long periods from a black-out hide built beside its nest chamber for the purposes of filming. It spent a good deal of time preening and walking around in the nest chamber, toying with small stones on the burrow floor and eyeing-up any beetle or spider which came its way. As it grew, it also liked to tromp down the tunnel to sit in a small alcove near the burrow entrance. From there, it could readily look out at the colony, getting a first taster, doubtless, of the social bustle which it may now be experiencing as an adult each summer.

Such unorthodox peeks into the underground life of puffins are now getting a boost from new technology. In the late 1990s, an enterprizing museum at Homer in Alaska set up a video link to a seabird colony on Gull Island. In addition to above-ground shots, this provided images from an infra-red camera recording in the near-darkness of a tufted puffin burrow.

Elsewhere, use of fiber-optic viewers called 'endoscopes' (conventionally employed for internal medical examination of people) has helped some researchers, such as RSPB seabird workers on Shetland, to keep an eye on the unfolding story of breeding success down a sample of Atlantic puffin burrows, without unduly worrying the burrow owners. Such high-tech gear can be a real boon, since puffins are quite sensitive to disturbance, especially during the incubation period.

Delivery of food can be rapid, with an adult appearing suddenly and dropping fish on the ground for the chick to pick up. However, chicks will also nibble at fish which are still in the adult's beak. In doing this, a chick's movements can be reminiscent of those made by an adult bird inviting another to begin a bout of billing. Such a link between food-begging and social/sexual behavior is not unusual in birds.

Although puffin chicks can be reared on a wide bill of fare, depending on colony location and the state of local food stocks, a few species of small, schooling fish crop up again and again in their diet. High in the feeding charts in both Atlantic and Pacific are sandeels, or 'sandlance' as they are termed in North America. Young stages of capelin can figure strongly in North America and Norway, with herring and sprats an energy-rich favorite in Britain and Iceland. Anchovies can top the bill for tufted puffins feeding in the Gulf of California. These shoaling species may occur in enormous numbers, but their presence in the ocean is patchy, so puffins have the challenge of locating the few shoals which may be accessible near the surface in a vast area of sea around the colonies.

A tufted puffin's streamlined power-dive.

Colony life itself may help in this daily hunt-the-shoal challenge. No one can be certain why most seabirds choose to breed in colonies. In some areas, a combination of fairly windblown land (good for giving uplift on take-off) on islands (free, in the past at least, from land-based predators) close to highly productive feeding grounds (near the continental shelf or otherwise stirred by strong, nutrient-mixing currents) may be part of the explanation. But being able to cash-in on the knowledge of other colony members is a further likely benefit.

When an accessible shoal is located, it is sometimes not long before the traffic of birds to and from shoal and colony becomes obvious as a 'flightline' to a human observer. Puffins, undoubtedly, will be even more attuned to such things and can watch and benefit, both from the mass movements of birds on flightlines and from the opportunities afforded by keeping a close eye on the neighbors.

All puffins have tough, backward-pointing spines on the roof of their mouth. Once a fish is caught, these resist its slippage and allow a big catch to be held.

Here, the classic puffin image — of a bird holding a tight-packed haul of small fry in its beak — could even give a useful clue to a neighbor about who would be worth following out to fishing grounds on the next journey.

Another apparent puzzle is how some puffins can arrange their catch in a regular head/tail/head/tail fashion. The most likely explanation is that this can happen when a puffin swims through a shoal at a time when all the fish are swimming in one direction (rather than scattering). If the puffin turns its head in a left/right/left/right sequence, a neatly alternating fish arrangement will result.

Even allowing for such tricks of the fisher's trade, the number of fish which a puffin can hold at one time is amazing, with loads of ten or so commonplace. More remarkable still, the biggest loads ever recorded for Atlantic puffins are virtually the same in three different countries: 61 in both Canada and Scotland and 'more than 60' in Norway. The downside of very large loads is that they comprise lots of small fish. Since the food value of typical prey fish selected by puffins declines very rapidly with decreasing length, large loads of tiddlers are almost useless to a growing chick. One 2 in- (5 cm-) sandeel is worth dozens of jellylike 1 in- (2.5 cm-) ones. The record Canadian 61-sandeel load weighed a mere fraction of an ounce (2.3 g); about the same as half a teaspoon of water, and about as little use to a growing puffin chick.

Tufted puffins tend to catch more small squid and shrimpy, invertebrate prey than horned or Atlantic puffins. Combined with their tendency to travel further out to sea from colonies than horned puffins (which often feed quite close to land) this difference in feeding behavior may again reflect a degree of competition between the two Pacific species.

The effort involved in food gathering may put a strain on the adults in some years. This was suggested by experiments on Atlantic puffins carried out on the Isle of May in the early 1990s by ornithologists Christine Wernham and

A good haul of young sandeels — favorite puffin prey.

David Bryant. Isle of May chicks which were given supplementary food received far fewer loads from their parents than chicks which did not get the free handouts (a drop from about three feeds a day to one feed in two to three days in one year of the experiment). The food-supplemented chicks

fledged earlier and in better condition than their counterparts, and in the following year, their parents (now without human help) enjoyed a much higher breeding success than un-manipulated pairs.

All this suggests that adult Atlantic puffins do incur personal costs from breeding effort, and that they may juggle their own long-term needs with the demands of any particular chick, especially in years when food is hard to find or of poor quality. On balance, this juggling might be more in the female's arena, since females deliver slightly more loads than males.

A study of Atlantic puffins in Newfoundland suggests, however, that males balance the extra care which females provide for young through incubation and chick-feeding by putting more effort into defence and maintenance of burrows.

If all goes well with the fishing and shrimping, chicks fledge after about one-and-a-half months. Atlantic and horned puffins both take roughly six weeks, tufted puffins a bit longer, with an average of 47 days recorded in the Gulf of Alaska and 50 days at Destruction Island in Washington State. Fledglings of all puffins leave alone and at night, and get no further help from their parents once they depart for the sea.

Puffin Conservation

A big challenge for foraging puffins is that good fish shoals may be in short supply in some years. Natural changes in the seas, such as the appearance from time to time of unusually cold or unusually warm water within fish spawning areas, can massively reduce the number of small fry available. Such events have had an impact on puffins in places including Newfoundland and California in recent decades.

Human activities can also take their toll. Oil pollution is the most widely publicized and visible manifestation of human-seabird conflict. But for puffins – which spend most of their lives well clear of land – oil has not, until now, been a serious threat, ghastly though it is for any individual which gets caught in a slick. There is no basis for complacency about this, since exploration of areas close to continental shelves, such as the so-called 'Atlantic Frontier' off northwest Britain and within feeding range of the huge St Kilda puffinries, could yet pose oil-related problems for puffins.

Killing by ground-based predators causes local difficulties. Foxes descended from fur-farm escapees are a problem on the Aleutians, and rats have been implicated in declines within parts of some British puffinries. Eradication of rats from the islands of Ailsa Craig and Handa in Scotland during the 1990s, masterminded by ornithologist Bernie Zonfrillo of Glasgow University (and coordinated by the Scottish Wildlife Trust on Handa), could yet coax puffins back to ground which they have not occupied for many years.

Particularly worrying during the last few decades has been the impact of commercial fisheries. In North America, tens of thousands of puffins in both Atlantic and Pacific have drowned after being snagged in nylon drift nets set to catch fish such as salmon. Most serious of all is the one-sided competition for prime puffin food stocks posed by so-called 'industrial' or 'biomass' fishing. This activity, which has also justifiably been called 'vacuuming the sea', involves the capture of fish not fit for human consumption. These are then processed to make fish oil and feedstuffs, such as meal which may be fed to livestock in farms on land and fishfarms in marine and fresh waters. Almost one-third of the world's annual catch of marine fish now comes from industrial fisheries. The boom in this market has been promoted by increased demand for cheap protein for use in intensive systems of agriculture.

In the North Sea, there has been a particularly dramatic turn-around since the 1940s, with a change from a fishery totally geared to human consumption to one where half the catch is now used as industrial raw material. For years, power stations in Denmark – the nation which exploits the bulk of the North Sea sandeel catch – even burnt oil derived from sandeels as a cheap alternative to more conventional fuel.

A possible threat to puffins and other seabirds from industrial fishing was highlighted in Shetland in the late 1980s, when tens of thousands of seabird chicks starved to death at a period when industrial fishing was at a peak there. Some scientists think that changes in sea currents could have contributed to the slump in Shetland's sandeels at that time. But following a temporary ban on that fishery and a subsequent re-opening on a very small scale, sandeel numbers have increased strongly again around Shetland and seabird breeding success has improved.

The strongest clue to the devastation which industrial fisheries may wreak on puffins comes from the Røst archipelago in Arctic Norway. Set at the end of the Lofoten Islands, the Røst puffinries are massive. Several hundred thousand puffins come here each year. The trouble is, in most years hardly any of them succeed in rearing a chick. Those chicks which hatch (and many pairs don't get as far as egg laying) usually starve at a few weeks old. My notes of a visit there, used in a feature produced with Frans Lanting for *National Geographic*, describe one of the casualties:

'Around me, hidden among shin-high tussocks of red fescue, are countless

Even the world's largest puffinries
can be badly hit by overfishing, so the spectacle
of a huge wheel in full whirl is both powerful and fragile.

As far as can be judged from
current studies, most puffin populations are in
good shape in both Pacific and Atlantic breeding areas.

burrows not unlike rabbit holes. They are puffin hatcheries. I reach deep into one and lift out a tiny body. An Arctic gust opens gaps in the chick's gray fluff, and I feel the chill of its feet against my palms. The bird, which hatched about a month ago, is one of thousands of baby puffins that have starved here already this year. I gently return the dead chick to the ground in the sad realization that soon every occupied burrow in the Røst archipelago will be a puffin tomb.

In the 1960s, a very intensive industrial fishery for spring-spawning herring took place here. The stocks – once part of the biggest fish resource in Europe – collapsed and the fishery closed. Decades later, long-term work carried out by ecologist Tycho Anker-Nilssen has shown that small herring are still hard to come by for the Røst puffins. Sea changes and big ups and downs of other fish populations have added to the instability. But all the signs are that it was lack of human restraint which sent the lethal ball into the skittles in the first place.

Away from such gloomy scenarios, the general state of puffindom has been healthy for several decades, with southward expansion of horned puffins, a small increase in tufted puffins in California and a marked upturn in Atlantic puffins in Britain. This is a very general comment, however, for most of the world's puffinries are not monitored at all, let alone watched on a regular basis. For many colonies, knowledge of numbers is not precise. This reflects the sheer difficulty of getting access to many auk breeding places, coupled with the physical challenges of working on ground which may be steep and tussocky, or covered in slippery boulders.

The solution to keeping a finger on the global puffin pulse is to carry out good, long-term monitoring of numbers, feeding and breeding success in parts of some colonies where access can be more or less guaranteed, year after year. And there's the rub. For it is notoriously difficult to get money for such projects, with many potential backers – government conservation agencies included – preferring short projects which run for a fixed term, then stop.

At a time of huge concern about warming global climate, changing conditions in the oceans, the health of fish stocks and the creatures which depend on them, the need is greater than ever for reliable facts and figures about species such as puffins. Yet all too often, governments are strong on rhetoric about 'sustainability' and weak on the funding of basic scientific work which could put some solid substance on the green jargon which has become the standard post-Earth-Summit bureaucrat-speak about environmental matters.

In recent years, work in Norway, Scotland and Newfoundland has shown that some seabirds, including puffins, can give vitally needed clues about fish stocks and marine conditions. They can be real indicators of sustainability, so it's vital that proper funds are directed to future studies of their fluctuating fortunes. Work in the U.S. by National Audubon Society seabird workers Steve Kress, Evie Weinstein and their helpers has further demonstrated that, with vision and determination, it is possible to restore communities of puffins and other seabirds damaged by previous human folly.

The huge interest in puffins by people world-wide does give hope that these superb birds will not be neglected, and that concern for them can help us to cherish the oceans which support both them and us. In most places, in most countries, where puffins breed within striking distance of human communities, jobs are sustained through summer trips around the puffinries. Businesses are also helped by puffin-linked tourists and by 'puffinabilia', with a local spin dreamed-up to provide mementoes for puffin-happy punters. Nowadays, you can also drop in on a growing number of puffin-related sites on the Internet to get facts, pictures and pure fanzine material on the north's most appealing auks.

If there is one thing I've learned in some quarter of a century of puffinology, it's that human enthusiasm for puffins is generally good news. It adds up to impetus for conservation, exciting personal challenges, memorable days and smiles on many faces. Long may it continue, and long may the tremendous trio thrive.

A timeless image of an icon of the seas.

*Quiet observation in a puffin
colony can be fascinating – for both
watcher and watched. There are still many things
left to discover about these familiar, yet mysterious birds.*

Atlantic Puffin

Scientific name	*Fratercula arctica*
Wing Length (mm) (average)	Males 162-185 Females 162-183
Weight (g) (average)	Welsh males 323-450 Svalbard males 620-710 Welsh females 300-433
Incubation Period	39 days
Chick Rearing	38-53 days
World Population estimate (breeding birds)	5-10 million

= breeding area   = normal winter range

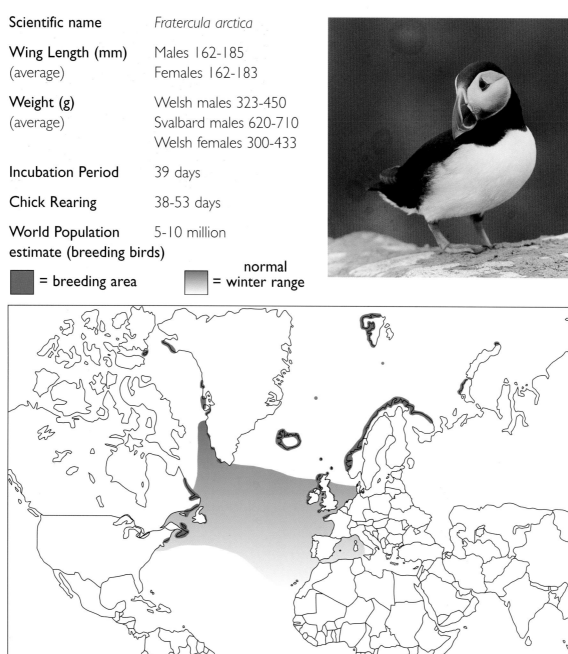

Horned Puffin

Scientific name	*Fratercula corniculata*
Wing Length (mm) (average)	Males 190-200 Females 186-197
Weight (g) (average)	Males 609-629 Females 581-618
Incubation Period	Roughly 41 days
Chick Rearing	37-46 days (42 average)
World Population estimate (breeding birds)	1.2 million

= breeding area   normal = winter range

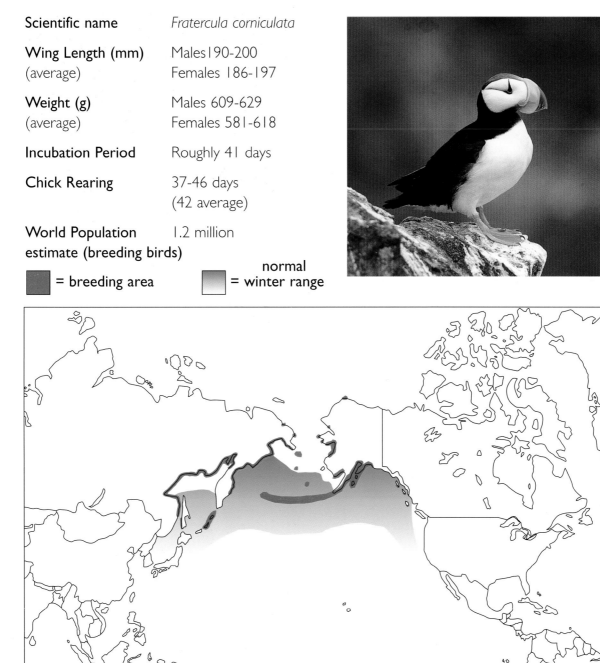

Tufted Puffin

Scientific name	*Fratercula cirrhata*
Wing Length (mm) (average)	204 in E. Aleutians (sexes combined)
Weight (g) (average)	Aleutian males 825 Aleutian females 778
Incubation Period	45 days
Chick Rearing	40-59 days (47 average) in Gulf of Alaska
World Population estimate (breeding birds)	More than 2 million

= breeding area

normal
= winter range

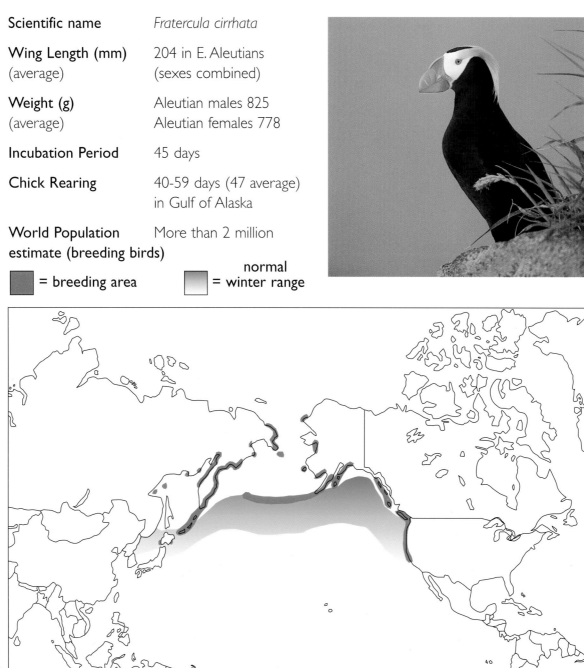

Recommended Reading

The Puffin by M.P. Harris, published in 1984 by T & A D Poyser, and still in print, is a trove of scientific facts and figures about the Atlantic puffin. My own *Puffins* (Whittet, 1993) also gives a general readership account of this species. It is worth searching second-hand bookshops and lists for Ronald Lockley's ground-breaking 1953 monograph *Puffins* (Dent) and Richard Perry's *Lundy, Isle of Puffins* (Lindsay Drummond, 1940).

For auks as a whole, including the trio of true puffins, state-of-the-art compendium is *The Auks* by Anthony J. Gaston, and Ian L. Jones, *Bird Families of the World* series, Oxford University Press, 1998.

People with access to the Internet can find some good sites by entering 'puffins' in their favorite search engine and then homing-in on web pages hosted by the Alaska Department of Fish and Game (strong on tufted and horned puffin facts) and the Canadian Wildlife Service (great for Atlantic puffins in their *Hinterland Who's Who* pages).

Biographical Note

Kenny Taylor is the Scottish Wildlife Trust's (SWT) Northern Regional Officer, covering the Highlands and Islands from a base at his family home on the Black Isle, close to the Moray Firth. Also a freelance writer and broadcaster, his writing on natural history, environmental news and wildlife photography appears nearly every month in *BBC Wildlife Magazine*. He has studied puffins and other auks at many major colonies in Britain, Arctic Norway (including Svalbard), the Faroes, Iceland, the U.S. and Canada since the mid-1970s, both for his own research, for the SWT's 'Operation Puffin' monitoring of puffin chicks and diet and for a variety of television, radio and magazine projects.

His doctoral studies of puffins and great black-backed gulls featured in *The Trials of Life* BBC TV series and formed the basis of the award-winning *Clowns of the Air* Wildlife on One BBC TV film on Atlantic puffins, for which he was scientific adviser. An assignment for *National Geographic* gave him a great opportunity to explore links between puffins and people in several countries, a subject which he is currently developing in a further project.

Index

*Entries in **bold** indicate pictures*